Jesus:
from Arrest to Ascension

Katherine Hilditch

'Jesus: from Arrest to Ascension'
by Katherine Hilditch
Copyright © 2015 Katherine Hilditch.
All Rights Reserved.

The Understanding Christianity Booklets

'How and Why Jesus Died'
by Katherine Hilditch
Copyright © 2014 Katherine Hilditch.
All Rights Reserved.

'Happy Easter!'
by Katherine Hilditch
Copyright © 2014 Katherine Hilditch.
All Rights Reserved.

'Why Jesus Went Back to Heaven'
by Katherine Hilditch
Copyright © 2014 Katherine Hilditch.
All Rights Reserved.

The Full Bible Accounts

'The Crucifixion'
compiled by Katherine Hilditch
Copyright © 2015 Katherine Hilditch.
All rights Reserved.

'The Resurrection'
compiled by Katherine Hilditch
Copyright © 2015 Katherine Hilditch.
All rights Reserved.

'The Ascension'
compiled by Katherine Hilditch
Copyright © 2015 Katherine Hilditch.
All rights Reserved.

In the booklets, unless otherwise indicated,
all Scripture quotations are taken from
the World English Bible British Edition (WEBBE)
(Any words in brackets are not in the original text
but are included to help understanding)

The full Bible accounts are all based on the WEBBE

Contents

Preface

Part 1	Booklet – 'How and Why Jesus Died'	Page 1
Part 2	Full Bible Account - The Crucifixion	Page 13
Part 3	Booklet – 'Happy Easter!'	Page 41
Part 4	Full Bible Account - The Resurrection	Page 51
Part 5	Booklet – 'Why Jesus Went Back to Heaven'	Page 69
Part 6	Full Bible Account - The Ascension	Page 81
Part 7	How to be Born-Again	Page 83

Preface

This book contains three booklets from my 'Understanding Christianity' series. Each booklet is followed by a section of my fully integrated Bible account of Jesus from His arrest to His ascension.

The Understanding Christianity Booklets
I'm a Christian and having spent many years both teaching and training people in the local church, I started writing booklets in 2013 to help people understand more about Christianity, whether they believe or not. Many people have been encouraged by them and found them really helpful. In the originals, each booklet has a section on being born-again. In this book, I have taken this section out of the individual booklets and put it separately at the end.

The Full Bible Accounts
I have often wanted to be able to read the full account of Jesus's last weeks on earth rather than in one Gospel at a time, so I set myself the task of integrating all four accounts into one narrative. I have used the World English Bible British Edition (WEBBE), which is copyright free, as my basis and have used exact wording form the Bible most of the time. But there are places where I needed to paraphrase or restructure sentences after amalgamating the accounts, to help the flow and aid understanding. I have also changed a few words to more modern ones. At the start of each section I have included the relevant Bible references.

Katherine Hilditch

Part 1

Understanding Christianity Booklet

How and Why Jesus Died

Jesus died on a cross which was a Roman form of capital punishment called crucifixion. It seemed the end of all hope for His followers and the end of a time of problems for others. It turned out to be neither.

Crucifixion

Crucifixion was the worst way of killing a person that the Romans could think of. A cross was formed out of two long pieces of wood, one laid across the other near the top to form the cross shape. The person's arms were stretched out along the horizontal sections and either tied to the cross or secured by driving a nail through the palm of each hand and into the wood. The feet were also either tied or nailed to the upright section of the cross. The cross was then lifted upright and slotted into a prepared hole in the ground. It was tall enough so no-one could reach up and set the person free. Jesus was nailed to the Cross.

Death by crucifixion took a long time, from hours to days, and was agonizing. Scholars have found that the actual resulting cause of death could be one or more of heart failure, hypovolemic shock, acidosis, asphyxia, arrhythmia, pulmonary embolism, or infection from the nail holes.

Sometimes, if death was taking too long, the Roman soldiers broke the legs of the person being crucified. This caused the whole weight of the body to hang from the arms. Breathing would quickly become impossible and the person would die. Jesus was crucified on the day before the Sabbath and the Jews wanted His body and those of the two criminals crucified with Him, to be taken down before sunset when the Sabbath would begin. The soldiers agreed to break their legs to hasten death, but when they came to Jesus they found he was already dead and did not need to.

The People's Reason for Killing Jesus

The people who killed Jesus wanted Him out of the way. The Jewish religious leaders saw Him as someone who was threatening their whole way of life, which was based on their religious laws, and they were worried about Him gathering new converts around Him in increasing numbers. The Romans who controlled the region at the time saw Him as a troublemaker.

For quite a while before His death, the Jewish leaders had been trying to catch Jesus out so they could take Him before their court and put Him on trial. Their main trick was to try and get Him to say or do something which was against their religious laws, but Jesus was always able to put them at a disadvantage instead. But eventually, with the help of one of Jesus's own disciples, Judas Iscariot, they arrested Him and put Him on trial.

He was passed back and forth between the Jewish leaders, King Herod and the Roman governor, Pontius Pilate. Pilate could not see how He had broken any law of the land, so he offered the crowd the choice of releasing Jesus or a murderer called Barabbas. This was the custom at the time of the Jews' Passover Feast. The crowd, at the religious leaders' insistence, shouted for Barabbas and when Pilate then asked them what he should do with Jesus, they shouted "Crucify Him!" Reluctantly Pilate agreed, but he ceremoniously washed his hands saying he was not accepting the blame for Jesus's death.

Pilate had handed Jesus over to the Roman soldiers who mocked Him by dressing Him in a kingly robe and putting a crown of thorns on His head and pretending to worship Him as King. Then they spat on Him and flogged Him. Putting His own clothes back on Him, they led Him out to crucify Him, along with two criminals.

God's Reason for the Crucifixion

The Jewish leaders and the Romans thought they were at last getting their own way, but Jesus's crucifixion had been planned by God, and Jesus was in control of it! He knew when it was God's perfect timing for it and He went of His own accord to Jerusalem and into the hands of His enemies. 1 John 3:8 gives one of God's reasons for it happening – *'To this end the Son of God was revealed: that he might destroy the works of the devil.'*

No-one can live a perfect life. Everyone does, says and thinks wrong things. You may feel you live a good life, but in your heart you know you still get some things wrong. You may be very aware that your life is far from good. Wrong actions, words and thoughts are called sin in the Bible. It is sin that stops people from having a loving, intimate relationship with God and it was the devil, or Satan, who first introduced sin into the world. God could never let sin go unpunished. He absolutely and totally hates it. So long before Jesus's birth, God gave His law to His people along with a system of sacrifices through which the people could receive His forgiveness for their sins. It's explained in detail in the Old Testament. Under this law everything depended on how people performed or measured up. If they obeyed the law perfectly then they were blessed, but if they disobeyed it in any way they were cursed. God wanted them to understand that they needed to avoid sin, but also that they could never be perfect. He wanted them to realise that they couldn't be perfect by their own effort and needed a saviour.

God loves you so much. He longs for you to know Him personally in a close Father and child relationship. He does not want to punish people. So He sent His Son Jesus, who never sinned once, to take the punishment for all people, for all sins and for all time. Hebrews 7:27 says Jesus - *'did this once for all, when he offered up himself.'* Jesus took all your sin, all your guilt and all your shame on Himself and He did it 'once for all'. He did it for all people - everyone who's ever lived and ever will live. He did it for all time - it stands in history at a specific time and will never need to be repeated. And He did it for all sins - past, present and future. Jesus was the final sacrifice. Jesus died instead of you! Jesus paid the price and suffered the punishment. And because of this, God's not angry with people anymore. You can now be at peace with God, free from the curse of the Old Testament law.

You are now free to come into that relationship with God which He longs for, not because you've earned it or deserve it, but because Jesus has done everything that is needed. When you become born-again, that is accept Jesus as your Lord and Saviour, you receive the total forgiveness He has won for you. Sin can no longer control you. You are set free from it. It doesn't mean you will live a perfect life. And it doesn't mean that sin doesn't matter. God still hates it, but He loves you and wants to help you live in a way that pleases Him which is the most fulfilling way to live. Satan would love you to keep on sinning so he can try to influence your life for the worse, but God has set you free to say "No" so your life can be lived for the best. When you do sin you can turn away from it, receive forgiveness and walk away free.

Jesus said in John 10:10 – *'The thief* (Satan) *only comes to steal, kill, and destroy.'* But his work is defeated. He will still try and influence things negatively, but now he cannot continue when Christians command him to go in the name of Jesus.

John 3:16 gives another of God's reasons for Jesus's death – *'For God so loved the world, that he gave his one and only Son, that whoever believes in him should not perish, but have eternal life.'* Jesus destroyed the works of Satan and because sin can no longer keep a born-again Christian out of God's presence, you can be sure, when you are born-again, that you will not perish, but live eternally with God in perfect joy and peace and love.

Now everything depends not on your performance, but on God's grace - His unconditional and undeserved love for you. It's not about what you do, it's all about what Jesus did and it all becomes reality in your life when you're born-again – that's amazingly good news! This is why Christians call the day of Jesus's crucifixion, 'Good Friday'.

Further Significance of the Cross

People were crucified publicly and it was an extremely shameful thing. But the Bible says in Hebrews 12:2 – *'for the joy that was set before him* (Jesus) *endured the cross, despising its shame.'* That joy came from knowing that what He was doing would make forgiveness, freedom, salvation, deliverance, prosperity and healing available to everyone who would accept Him as their Lord and Saviour.

Death itself was defeated when Jesus died on the Cross. 2 Timothy 1:10 says Jesus – *'abolished death, and brought life and immortality to light.'* This was perfectly demonstrated when Jesus came back to life three days later.

Through His suffering, sickness is defeated and healing is available for all who believe. 1 Peter 2:24 says - *'by whose stripes* (wounds) *you were healed.'*

God also won true prosperity through Jesus. 2 Corinthians 8:9 says – *'He was rich, yet for your sake He became poor, so that you through His poverty might become rich.'* This isn't about having millions of pounds, an extravagant lifestyle, a huge house and many expensive possessions. It is about having enough to live without any struggle and without the fear and stress of financial problems, and also with enough over to be able to give into God's Kingdom, and help and bless others. What a blessing to know that God can and wants to look after all your needs.

Victory!

The Cross was the place where victory was won over Satan and all his works of death, sin, sickness, poverty and bondage. Jesus's last words which He cried out just before He died were "It is finished." He had done the work God sent Him to do and He had done it perfectly and completely. Things would never be the same again. From that point in time everyone has the free opportunity to start to walk in the victory Jesus won for them on the Cross and that includes you!

Some amazing things happened as Jesus finally died. Matthew 27:51 says - *'the veil of the temple was torn in two from the top to the bottom.'* This is hugely significant. The veil in the temple of the Jews separated the area called the Holy of Holies from the rest of the temple. Only the high priest was allowed to go beyond the curtain into God's holy presence and only once a year. As Jesus died the curtain was miraculously ripped from top to bottom demonstrating beyond doubt that now anyone who trusted in Jesus could come straight into God's presence just as they are and wherever they are. You no longer need to go through a priest to gain access to God. The way is open and available to you directly. Just you and God – wow!

And Matthew 27:52 goes on to say that - *'The earth quaked and the rocks were split. The tombs were opened, and many bodies of the saints who had fallen asleep were raised.'* Matthew 27:54 then says – *'Now the* (Roman) *centurion, and those who were with him watching Jesus, when they saw the earthquake, and the things that were done, feared exceedingly, saying, "Truly this was the Son of God."'* Through the Cross you can be assured of victory in this life and through eternity as you receive Jesus as your Lord and Saviour.

The Power of the Cross

The Cross stands at the centre of everything. It is the most powerful thing that has ever happened in history and its power is as real today. That power comes into your life when you become born-again. You can start to walk in an intimate loving relationship with your Father God, experiencing forgiveness, freedom, victory, healing and eternal life, lacking nothing and filled with Jesus's Holy Spirit.

The Bible Account

There is an account of Jesus's crucifixion in each of the four gospels in the Bible. To some degree the different gospels focus on different aspects of what happened and include different details. In part 2, I have integrated the four accounts into one narrative, so you can read the full detailed story.

Part 2

Full Bible Account

The Crucifixion

The Full Bible Account of Jesus's Arrest, Trials, Death and Burial

Matthew 26:46-75, 27:1-66
Mark 14:42-72, 15:1-47
Luke 22:47-71, 23:1-56
John 18:3-40, 19:1-42
Acts 1:18-20

Introduction

Jesus has shared his last meal with his disciples. But afterwards, one of them, Judas Iscariot, went to the chief priests who wanted to kill Jesus, and told them where they could find him so they could arrest him. They paid Judas thirty pieces of silver for the information. The account starts as the soldiers and officers arrive in the Garden of Gethsemane where Jesus has been praying while his disciples were sleeping nearby.

Jesus is Arrested

Matthew 26:46-56; Mark 14:42-52; Luke 22:47-53; John 18:3-11

Jesus, knowing Judas was approaching, said to his disciples, "Arise, let's be going. See, he who betrays me is at hand." Immediately, while he was still speaking, Judas came leading a very large detachment of soldiers and officers from the chief priests, the scribes, and the elders. They brought lanterns, torches, swords and clubs with them. Jesus, knowing all the things that were to happen to him, went out to them.

Now Judas had given the soldiers a sign, saying, "The one I kiss, that is he. Seize him, and lead him away safely." Judas immediately came to Jesus and said, "Rabbi! Rabbi!" and kissed him. Jesus said to him, "Judas, friend, why are you here? Do you betray the Son of Man with a kiss?"

Jesus said to the multitude, "Who are you looking for?" They answered him, "Jesus of Nazareth." He said to them, "I am he." When he said to them, "I am he," they went backward, and fell to the ground. He asked them again, "Who are you looking for?" They said, "Jesus of Nazareth." Jesus answered, "I told you that I am he. If therefore, you seek me, let these others go their way." He said this so that the word might be fulfilled which he had spoken, "Of those whom you have given me, I have lost none."

When his disciples who stood by saw what was about to happen, they said to Jesus, "Lord, shall we strike with the sword?" And one of them, Simon Peter, stretched out his hand, and having a sword, drew it, and struck the high priest's servant, cutting off his right ear. The servant's name was Malchus. Then Jesus said to Peter, "Put your sword back into its sheath, for all those who take the sword will die by the sword. Do you think that I couldn't ask my

Father, and he would even now send me more than twelve legions of angels? But if that happened, how would the Scriptures be fulfilled that say it must this way? The cup which the Father has given me, shall I not surely drink it?" And Jesus said, "Let me at least do this"—and he touched Malchus's ear and healed him.

Jesus said to the multitude of chief priests, captains of the temple, and the elders, who had come against him, "Have you come out as against a robber with swords and clubs to seize me? When I was with you in the temple teaching daily, you didn't stretch out your hands against me and arrest me. But all this has happened that the Scriptures of the prophets might be fulfilled. This is your hour, and the power you use is the power of darkness."

Then the soldiers came and laid hands on Jesus, and seized him and all the disciples left him, and fled.

But one young man followed him. He only had a linen cloth thrown around himself over his naked body. When the young men grabbed him by the cloth, he let it go and fled from them naked.

Jesus before Annas

Matthew 26:57; Mark 14:53; Luke 22:54;
John 18:12-14,19-24

The commanding officer, the officers of the Jews and the whole detachment of soldiers seized Jesus and bound him. They led him first to Annas who was one of the high priests that year along with his son-in-law, Caiaphas. It was Caiaphas who had advised the Jews that it was better that one man should die instead of the people.

Annas therefore asked Jesus about his disciples, and about his teaching. Jesus answered him, "I spoke openly to the world. I always taught in synagogues and in the temple where the Jews always meet. I said nothing in secret. Why do you ask me? Ask those who have heard me what I said to them. They know the things which I said." When he had said this, one of the officers standing by slapped Jesus with his hand, saying, "Do you answer the high priest like that?" Jesus answered him, "If I have spoken evil, explain why it is evil; but if I have spoken well, why do you beat me?"

Annas ordered Jesus to be sent bound to Caiaphas. Those who had arrested Jesus seized him and led him away and brought him into the high priest's house. All the chief priests, the elders, and the scribes came with him. Simon Peter and John, two of Jesus's disciples, followed him from a distance to the court of the high priest.

Peter Denies He Knows Jesus

Matthew 26:58,69-70; Mark 14:54,66-68; Luke 22:54-57; John 18:15-18,25

Now John was known to the high priest, and went with Jesus into the court of the high priest; but Peter stood at the door outside. So John went out and spoke to the maid who was watching at the door, and brought Peter in.

The servants and the officers were standing in the courtyard, having made a fire of coals in the middle of it, for it was cold, and they were warming themselves. Peter stood with them, warming himself in the light of the fire. He then sat down with the officers, to see how Jesus's trial ended. As he was sitting in the courtyard outside the court, the maid who kept the door saw Peter in the firelight and came to him. She looked intently at him and said, "You were also with Jesus, the Galilean! Are you one of this Nazarene's disciples?" But he denied Jesus before them all, saying, "Woman, I am not. I neither know, nor understand what you are talking about." He went out on the porch, and the rooster crowed.

Jesus before Caiaphas
Matthew 26:59-68; Mark 14:55-65; Luke 22:63-65

Now the chief priests, the elders, and the whole council tried to find witnesses who would give false testimony against Jesus, so that they could put him to death. Even though many false witnesses came forward, their testimonies did not agree with each other, so they found none. But at last two false witnesses came forward and gave false testimony against him, saying, "We heard this man say, 'I am able to destroy the temple of God that is made with hands, and I will do so, and in three days I will build another made without hands.'" But even then their testimonies did not agree.

The high priest stood up in the middle and said to Jesus, "Have you no answer? What is this that these people testify against you?" But Jesus stayed quiet, and answered nothing. Again the high priest asked him, "I charge you under oath by the living God, that you tell us whether you are the Christ, the Son of God, the Blessed?" Jesus said to him, "You have said it. I am. Nevertheless, I tell you, after this you will see the Son of Man sitting at the right hand of the power of God, and coming on the clouds of the sky."

Then the high priest tore his clothing, saying, "He has spoken blasphemy! Why do we need any more witnesses? Behold, now you have heard his blasphemy, what do you think?" They all condemned him, saying, "He is worthy of death!"

Some began to spit on him and, after they had blindfolded him, the men who held Jesus mocked him and beat him with their fists, striking him on the face. The officers slapped him with the palms of their hands, saying, "Prophesy to us, you Christ! Who is the one who struck you?" They spoke many other things against him, insulting him.

Peter Denies Jesus Twice More
Matthew 26:71-75; Mark 14:69-71; Luke 22:58-62; John 18:26-27

A little while after Peter had gone out onto the porch, the maid saw him again, and began again to tell those who stood by, "This man also was with Jesus of Nazareth." One of the servants of the high priest, being a relative of the soldier whose ear Peter had cut off, saw him, and said to him, "Didn't I see you in the garden with Jesus? You aren't also one of his disciples, are you? You are one of them!" Again Peter denied it with an oath and answered, "Man, I am not! I don't know the man."

After about one hour had passed, again those who stood by came and confidently said to Peter, "Surely you truly are also one of them, for you are a Galilean and your speech shows it." Then Peter began to curse and to swear and denied it again saying, "Man, I don't know what you are talking about! I don't know this man of whom you speak!" Immediately, while he was still speaking, the rooster crowed the second time.

The Lord Jesus turned and looked at Peter. Then Peter remembered the word which Jesus had said to him, "Before the rooster crows twice, you will deny me three times." When he remembered this, he went out and wept bitterly.

Full Bible Account – The Crucifixion

Jesus before Caiaphas and the Council
Matthew 27:1; Mark 15:1; Luke 22:66-71

Now as soon as morning had come, the whole council of the elders of the people, both the chief priests and the scribes, gathered together and held a consultation against Jesus to put him to death.

They led Jesus into their council, saying, "If you are the Christ, tell us." But he said to them, "If I tell you, you won't believe, and if I ask, you will never answer me or let me go. From now on, the Son of Man will be seated at the right hand of the power of God." They all said, "Are you then the Son of God?" He said to them, "You say it, because I am." They said, "Why do we need any more witness? For we ourselves have heard from his own mouth!"

Jesus before the Roman Governor, Pilate
Matthew 27:2,11-14; Mark 15:1; Luke 23:1-7; John 18:28-38

The council bound Jesus, and the whole company of them rose up and led him away from Caiaphas into the Praetorium and delivered him up to Pontius Pilate, the governor. They themselves didn't enter into the Praetorium, so that they would not be defiled and not be able to eat the Passover. Pilate therefore went out to them, and said, "What accusation do you bring against this man Jesus?" They answered him, "If this man weren't an evildoer, we wouldn't have delivered him up to you." And they began to accuse Jesus, saying, "We found this man perverting the nation, forbidding paying taxes to Caesar, and saying that he himself is Christ, a king."

Pilate therefore entered again into the Praetorium, called Jesus, and when he stood before him, said to him, "Are you the King of the Jews?" Jesus said to him, "So you say. Do you say this by yourself, or did others tell you about me?" Pilate answered, "I'm not a Jew, am I? Your own nation and the chief priests delivered you to me. What have you done?" Jesus answered, "My Kingdom is not of this world. If my Kingdom were of this world, then my servants would fight, so that I wouldn't be delivered to the Jews. But now my Kingdom is not from here." Pilate therefore said to him, "Are you a king then?" Jesus answered, "You say that I am a king. For this reason I have been born, and for this reason I have come into the world, that I should testify to the truth. Everyone who is of the truth listens to my voice." Pilate said to him, "What is truth?"

When he had said this, Pilate went out again to the chief priests, the elders and the multitudes. The chief priests and elders accused Jesus of many things, but he answered nothing. Then Pilate said to him, "Don't you hear how many things they testify against you?" Pilate again asked him, "Have you no answer?" Jesus gave him no answer, not even one word, so that Pilate marvelled greatly.

Pilate said to the Jews, "I find no basis for a charge against this man. Take him yourselves, and judge him according to your law." They said to him, "It is not lawful for us to put anyone to death," This was said so that the word of Jesus might be fulfilled which he spoke signifying by what kind of death he should die. And they insisted, saying, "He stirs up the people, teaching throughout all Judea, beginning from Galilee even to this place."

But when Pilate heard Galilee mentioned, he asked if Jesus was a Galilean. When he found out that he was in Herod's jurisdiction, he sent him to Herod, who was also in Jerusalem during those days.

Jesus before King Herod
Luke 23:8-12

Now when Herod saw Jesus, he was exceedingly glad, for he had wanted to see him for a long time, because he had heard many things about him. He hoped to see some miracle done by him. He questioned him with many words, but Jesus gave no answers. The chief priests and the scribes stood vehemently accusing him.

Herod with his soldiers humiliated him and mocked him, dressing him in luxurious clothing, and they sent him back to Pilate. Herod and Pilate became friends with each other that very day, for before that they were enemies.

Jesus Before Pilate a Second Time
Luke 23:13-16

Pilate called together the chief priests and the rulers and the people and said to them, "You brought this man to me as one that perverts the people, and see, I have examined him before you, and found no basis for a charge against this man concerning those things of which you accuse him. Neither has Herod, for I sent you to him, and see, nothing worthy of death has been done by him. I will therefore chastise him and release him."

Jesus is Tortured
Matthew 27:27-31; Mark 15:16-19; John 19:1-3

So Pilate took Jesus, and flogged him. Then the governor's soldiers took Jesus into the Praetorium and gathered the whole garrison together against him. They stripped him and dressed him in a purple garment and put a scarlet robe on him. The soldiers twisted thorns into a crown, and put it on his head and a reed in his right hand. They knelt down before him, and mocking him, they began to salute him, saying, "Hail, King of the Jews!" They kept saying it. They spat on him and took the reed and struck him on the head and kept slapping him.

Jesus Continues Before Pilate
Matthew 27:15-26; Mark 15:6-15,20; Luke 23:17-25; John 18:39-40,19:2-16

Then Pilate went out again to the Jews and said to them, "Behold the man! I bring him out to you that you may know that I find no basis for a charge against him." Jesus therefore came out wearing the crown of thorns and the purple garment. When the chief priests and the officers of the Jews saw him, they shouted, "Crucify! Crucify!" Pilate said to them, "Take him yourselves, and crucify him, for I find no basis for a charge against him." The Jews answered him, "We have a law, and by our law he ought to die, because he made himself the Son of God." When Pilate heard them say this, he was more afraid.

He entered into the Praetorium again, and said to Jesus, "Where are you from?" But Jesus gave him no answer. Pilate therefore said to him, "Aren't you speaking to me? Don't you know that I have power to release you, and have power to crucify you?" Jesus answered, "You would have no power at all against me, unless it were given to you from above. Therefore he who delivered me to you has greater sin."

At this, Pilate was seeking to release him, but the Jews cried out, saying, "If you release this man, you aren't Caesar's friend! Everyone who makes himself a king speaks against Caesar!" When Pilate heard these words, he brought Jesus out, and sat down on the judgment seat at a place called "The Pavement", which was 'Gabbatha' in Hebrew. Now it was about the sixth hour on the Preparation Day of the

Passover.

While he was sitting on the judgment seat, his wife sent a message to him, saying, "Have nothing to do with that righteous man, for I have suffered many things today in a dream because of him."

The Romans had then a notable prisoner called Barabbas. He was a robber and had been thrown into prison for a revolt in the city, during which he had committed murder. He was bound with his fellow insurgents. Now at the feast the governor was accustomed to release to the multitude one prisoner, whoever they asked for.

Therefore when they were gathered together, Pilate said to the Jews, "You have a custom, that I should release someone to you at the Passover." The multitude, crying aloud, began to ask him to do this just as he always did. He asked, "Which of the two do you want me to release to you? Barabbas, or Jesus, the King of the Jews who is called Christ?" For he perceived that the chief priests had delivered Jesus up to him out of envy. Now the chief priests and the elders stirred up the multitude and persuaded them to ask him to release

Full Bible Account – The Crucifixion

Barabbas to them, and destroy Jesus. They all cried out together, shouting, "Away with this man! Release to us Barabbas!"

Pilate, wanting to release Jesus, said to them, "What then shall I do to Jesus, who is called Christ, whom you call the King of the Jews?" They all cried out to him, "Let him be crucified!" Pilate said to them, "Why, what evil has he done?" But they shouted again, crying out exceedingly, "Crucify him! Crucify him!" But Pilate, the governor said to them the third time, "Why? What evil has this man done? I have found no capital crime in him." But they cried out urgently with loud voices, saying, "Let him be crucified! Away with him! Away with him! Crucify him!" Pilate said to them, "Shall I crucify your King?" The chief priests answered, "We have no king but Caesar!" The voices of the multitude and of the chief priests prevailed.

So when Pilate saw that nothing was being gained, but rather that a disturbance was starting, he took water and washed his hands before the multitude, saying, "I am innocent of the blood of this righteous person. You see to it." All the people answered, "May his blood be on us, and on our children!"

So Pilate, wishing to please the multitude, decreed that what they asked for should be done. He released to them the one they wanted - Barabbas, who had been thrown into prison for insurrection and murder, and he handed Jesus over to their will to be crucified. The soldiers took the purple off him, and put his own garments on him and the Jews took him away to crucify him.

Judas's Death
Matthew 27:3-10; Acts 1:18-20

When Judas, who had betrayed him, saw that Jesus was condemned, he felt remorse, and brought back the thirty pieces of silver to the chief priests and elders, saying, "I have sinned in that I betrayed innocent blood." But they said, "What is that to us? You see to it." He threw down the pieces of silver in the sanctuary, and departed. Now he had obtained a potter's field with the reward for his wickedness. There he hanged himself, and falling headlong his body burst open and all his intestines gushed out. In their language, that field became known to everyone who lived in Jerusalem as 'Akeldama,' that is, 'the field of blood.' And it is still known so today. It is written in the book of Psalms, 'Let his habitation be made desolate. Let no one dwell therein;' and, 'Let another take his office.'

The chief priests took the pieces of silver, and said, "It's not lawful to put them into the treasury, since it is the price of blood." They took counsel, and bought the potter's field with the silver pieces, to bury strangers in. Then that which was spoken through Jeremiah the prophet was fulfilled, saying, "They took the thirty pieces of silver, the price which some of the children of Israel had put upon him, and they used them to buy the potter's field, as the Lord commanded me."

The Walk to Golgotha
Matthew 27:32; Mark 15:21; Luke 23:26-32; John 19:16-17

The Jews took Jesus and led him away. He went out, carrying his cross. As they came out, they grabbed a man coming from the country, whose name was Simon of Cyrene, the father of Alexander and Rufus, and they forced him to go with them, so that he might carry Jesus's cross. They laid it on him, to carry it following after Jesus.

A great multitude of the people followed, including women who also mourned and lamented him. But Jesus, turning to them, said, "Daughters of Jerusalem, don't weep for me, but weep for yourselves and for your children. For behold, the days are coming in which they will say, 'Blessed are the barren, the wombs that never bore, and the breasts that never nursed.' Then they will begin to tell the mountains, 'Fall on us!' and tell the hills, 'Cover us.' For if they do these things when the tree is green, what will be done when it is dry?" They also led two criminals out with him to be put to death.

Jesus is Crucified

Matthew 27:33-49; Mark 15:22-36; Luke 23:33-44; John 19:17-29

When they had brought Jesus to the place called Golgotha, which is, being interpreted from Hebrew, 'The place of a skull', they offered him sour wine mixed with gall and myrrh to drink, but when he had tasted it he would not drink.

It was the third hour, and when they had crucified him there, Jesus said, "Father, forgive them, for they don't know what they are doing."

Then the soldiers took his garments and divided them into four parts and gave one part to each soldier. But his coat was seamless, woven from the top throughout, so they said to one another, "Let's not tear it, but cast lots for it to decide whose it will be." This fulfilled the Scripture which says, "They parted my garments amongst them. For my cloak they cast lots." Then the soldiers sat and watched Jesus while the people stood watching too.

Pilate wrote the accusation against him and the soldiers put it on the cross over his head. It said, "THIS IS JESUS OF NAZARETH, THE KING OF THE JEWS." Many of the Jews read it, for the place where Jesus was crucified was near the city and it was written in Hebrew, in Latin, and in Greek. The chief priests of the Jews therefore said to Pilate, "Don't write, 'The King of the Jews,' but, 'he said, "I am King of the Jews."'" Pilate answered, "What I have written, I have written."

They crucified the two criminals who were robbers with him; one on his right hand and one on his left with Jesus in the middle. Thus the Scripture was fulfilled, which says, "He was counted with transgressors."

Those who passed by blasphemed him, wagging their heads and saying, "Ha! You who would destroy the temple, and build it in three days, if you are the Son of God, save yourself and come down from the cross!" Likewise the chief priests also scoffed at him mocking him amongst themselves with the scribes, Pharisees, and the elders saying, "He trusts in God. Let God deliver him now, if he wants him; for he said, 'I am the Son of God.' He saved others. If he is the King of Israel, the Christ of God, his chosen one, let him come down from the cross now and save himself that we may see and will believe in him. But he can't do it." The soldiers also mocked him, coming to him and offering him vinegar, and saying, "If you are the King of the Jews, save yourself!"

One of the robbers who were crucified with him also insulted him, saying, "If you are the Christ, save yourself and us!" But the other robber answered, and rebuking him said, "Don't you even fear God, seeing you are under the same condemnation? And we indeed justly, for we receive the due reward for our deeds, but this man has done nothing wrong." He said to Jesus, "Lord, remember me when you come into your Kingdom." Jesus said to him, "Assuredly I tell you, today you will be with me in Paradise."

Standing by the cross of Jesus were his mother, his mother's sister, Mary the wife of Clopas, and Mary Magdalene. When Jesus saw his mother and John, the disciple whom he loved, standing there, he said to his mother, "Woman, behold, your son!" Then he said to John, "Behold, your mother!" From that hour, John took her to his own home.

It was now about the sixth hour, and darkness came over the whole land until the ninth hour. At about the ninth hour Jesus cried with a loud voice, saying, "Eloi, Eloi, lama sabachthani?" which is, being interpreted, "My God, my God, why have you forsaken me?" Some of them who stood there, when they heard it, said, "This man is calling Elijah."

After this, Jesus, seeing that everything was now finished, that the Scripture might be fulfilled, said, "I am thirsty." Now a vessel full of vinegar was standing there, so immediately one of them ran, took a sponge, filled it with vinegar, put it on a reed of hyssop, and held it to his mouth for him to drink. The others said, "Let him be. Let's see whether Elijah comes to take him down and save him."

Jesus Dies

Matthew 27:50-56; Mark 15:37-41; Luke 23:45-49; John 19:30-37

When Jesus had received the vinegar, he said, "It is finished." He cried out with a loud voice, "Father, into your hands I commit my spirit!" Having said this, he breathed his last and gave up his spirit. The sun was darkened, and the veil of the temple was torn in two from the top to the bottom. The earth quaked and the rocks were split. The tombs were opened, and many bodies of the saints who had fallen asleep were raised and came out of the tombs three days later, after his resurrection, and entered into the holy city and appeared to many.

When the centurion, who stood by opposite Jesus, and those who were with him saw the earthquake and the other things that happened, and that he cried out like this and breathed his last, they feared exceedingly. The centurion glorified God, saying, "Certainly this was a righteous man. Truly this man was the Son of God!"

It was the Preparation Day, and so that the bodies wouldn't remain on the cross on the Sabbath (for that Sabbath was a special one), the Jews asked Pilate that their legs might be broken, and that their bodies might be taken down. So the soldiers came and broke the legs of the first robber and of the other one who was crucified with Jesus; but when they came to Jesus, and saw that he was already dead, they didn't break his legs. However one of the soldiers pierced his side with a spear, and immediately blood and water came out. These things happened that the Scripture might be fulfilled, "A bone of him will not be broken." Again another Scripture says, "They will look on him whom they pierced." John has seen and testifies to all this, and his testimony is true. He knows that he tells the truth, that you may believe.

When the multitudes that came together to see the crucifixion, saw the things that were done, returned home beating their breasts. All his acquaintances and many women who had followed Jesus from Galilee to Jerusalem, including those who had served him, stood at a distance watching everything. Amongst them were Mary Magdalene, Mary the mother of James the less, Joses and Salome, the mother of the sons of Zebedee.

Jesus's Burial is Arranged
Matthew 27:57-58; Mark 15:42-45; Luke 23:50-52; John 19:38

After these things, when evening had come, because it was the Preparation Day, that is the day before the Sabbath, a rich man named Joseph came. Joseph was from Arimathaea, a city of the Jews. He was a prominent council member who was also a disciple of Jesus, but in secret for fear of the Jews, and he was waiting for God's Kingdom. He was a good and righteous man and had not consented to the council's decision and actions.

He boldly went in to Pilate, and asked for Jesus' body. Pilate marvelled that Jesus was already dead; and summoning the centurion, he asked him whether he had been dead long. When he found out from the centurion, he gave Joseph permission to take the body and commanded that it be given to him.

Jesus is Buried
Matthew 27:9-61; Mark 15:46-47; Luke 23:53-56;
John 19:38-42

It was the day of the Preparation, and the Sabbath was drawing near, so Joseph came and took down Jesus' body. Nicodemus, who had first came to Jesus by night, also came bringing a mixture of myrrh and aloes, weighing about a hundred Roman pounds. They took his body and bound it in a clean linen cloth with the spices, as the custom of the Jews is when they bury a body.

Now in the place where he was crucified there was a garden. In the garden was Joseph's own new tomb, which he had cut out in the rock. No-one had ever been laid in it. So because of the Jews' Preparation Day they laid Jesus there, as it was nearby. Joseph rolled a great stone against the door of the tomb, and departed.

The women, including Mary Magdalene and Mary, the mother of Joses, who had come with him out of Galilee, followed after, and sitting opposite the tomb, saw how his body was laid there. They returned home and prepared spices and ointments. On the Sabbath they rested according to the commandment.

The Romans Secure the Tomb
Matthew 27:62-66

Also on the next day, the chief priests and the Pharisees gathered together and said to Pilate, "Sir, we remember what that deceiver said

Full Bible Account – The Crucifixion

while he was still alive: 'After three days I will rise again.' Command therefore that the tomb be made secure until the third day, lest perhaps his disciples come at night and steal him away, and tell the people, 'He is risen from the dead;' and the last deception will be worse than the first." Pilate said to them, "You have a guard. Go; make it as secure as you can." So they went with the guard and made the tomb secure, sealing the stone.

Part 3

Understanding Christianity Booklet

Happy Easter!

Ask children what Easter makes them think of and most of them will probably say "Easter eggs". But Easter is actually a celebration of an amazingly wonderful and powerful day in history, when Jesus, having been killed on a cross, came back to life. Customs involving chocolate, eggs, bunnies, bonnets and hot cross buns abound through the world, but they are incidental to the real meaning of Easter.

What Happened?

When Jesus's body had been taken down from the Cross a man called Joseph took it and buried it in his own empty tomb in a garden. Jesus's enemies were pleased that they had got rid of Him at last. But the Jewish religious leaders started to worry in case any of Jesus's followers should steal the body and pretend He had come back to life. So they went to the Roman governor, Pilate, and asked him to make the tomb secure. He gave them permission to do so and also provided soldiers to guard it. They sealed a huge stone in front of the tomb and left the soldiers on guard. The next day was the Sabbath when no Jews worked, so Jesus's followers did not go to the tomb until the following day.

First there was a huge earthquake and the stone rolled away from the door of the tomb. The soldiers were so afraid they fell to the ground as though they were dead. The first people to visit the tomb were some of the women who had been Jesus's followers. They had gone to put spices on the body as was the custom and were surprised to find the tomb open. They went in and found Jesus's body had gone. An angel was there who told them He had risen from the dead. But one of the women was distraught that the body had gone and stood crying in the garden. A man, who she presumed was the gardener, asked her why she was crying and who she was looking for. She explained and He said her name, "Mary." She then realised it was Jesus Himself. The women went to tell the rest of Jesus's followers. Some of them rushed to the tomb and found what the women said was true. Jesus's coming back to life from the dead is called the resurrection.

He appeared to His followers over the next days and weeks many times, helping them to understand what had happened and reassuring them.

Did It Really Happen?

Jesus did exist. Writings from the time, other than the Bible, tell of Him, and historically record His death by crucifixion. It is also undeniably true that the tomb was empty and the body was never found.

John was one of Jesus's original twelve

followers or disciples. He wrote the gospel of John and his account of Jesus's life, work, death and resurrection is first hand. In John 20:31 he says – *'these are written, that you may believe that Jesus is the Christ, the Son of God, and that believing you may have life in his name.'* John, along with Jesus's other close followers, was completely shaken and in despair after Jesus's death. But he went on to write his gospel, declaring that Jesus was indeed God and that He had risen from the dead. He could only have done that if he was absolutely convinced. He was, because he had seen Jesus alive again with his own eyes.

No-one could produce the body to 'prove' that Jesus hadn't come back to life. So sceptics say that it was stolen. The Jewish religious leaders at the time bribed the Roman soldiers to say Jesus's followers had stolen the body. This is the most common theory put forward today. But probably the most compelling reason for believing in the resurrection is the change in Jesus's followers. After the crucifixion they were in despair and frightened, but having met with Jesus after He came back to life, were completely transformed. Matthew 28:19-20 says that one of the last things He said to them before He went back to heaven was – *'Go, and make disciples of all nations, baptizing them in the name of the Father and of the Son and of the Holy Spirit, teaching them to observe all things that I commanded you. Behold, I am with you always, even to the end of the age.'* And this is what they did. They went on to put themselves in great danger preaching and spreading the truth of Jesus and there is historical evidence that many of them were killed for their belief. Would someone who knew the resurrection was a sham be willing to suffer torture and death for it? No! And if Jesus never came back to life, what is the historical explanation for the spread of Christianity? What would have made orthodox Jews change the religious ways of centuries and risk everything to tell others about Him? Also many ordinary believers were and still are willing to take great risks in order to meet together to learn about Jesus and worship Him.

Some people accept the resurrection, but say Jesus's body didn't come back to life, just His spirit. After His resurrection, Jesus ate fish with His followers. In his gospel, Matthew tells how people grabbed at His feet. His actual body had been brought back to life and transformed by God into an eternal one.

It has been suggested that those who saw Jesus were hallucinating, but so many people met with Jesus after His resurrection and their accounts all agree. This could never happen even if every person who saw Him was hallucinating at the time. A hallucination is completely individual to the person experiencing it. The gospels record fifteen different appearances of Jesus to lots of different people - there were five hundred people at one time and just one or two at others. And after Jesus went back to heaven a few weeks later, there were no more accounts of appearances. Had all those people stopped hallucinating as quickly as they had started?!

Another theory is that Jesus wasn't actually dead when He was put in the tomb and got out Himself. But during His trial, Jesus had been scourged. This Roman method of torture consisted of Jesus being hit by a minimum of six men using brass knuckledusters, followed by His back being whipped with a whip made up of many leather thongs into which bits of bone and metal had been fastened. This sliced through skin, muscle, blood vessels including arteries and into body organs. It was only stopped when the victim was nearly dead. Jesus also had a crown of thorns rammed onto

His head and had a further beating with a rod. The soldiers tried to get Him to carry His own cross to the place of execution, but He was physically incapable and someone else had to do it for Him. He was nailed to the Cross through His hands and feet and left to hang and die. How could someone who had endured all this survive? After He had died a soldier drove a spear into His side and blood and water came out – this showed that He was indeed dead and the experienced Roman soldiers confirmed this. He was then laid in the tomb. Such a severely damaged man could not have survived for long lying on a cold stone slab. And even if He had survived all that, would He have had the strength to push the huge sealed stone away from the doorway and fight off the Roman soldiers?

How much simpler to just believe!

Why Was the Resurrection Essential?

The resurrection finally proved once and for all that Jesus was the Son of God. Romans 1:4 says Jesus – *'was declared to be the Son of God with power, according to the Spirit of holiness, by the resurrection from the dead.'*

Jesus's resurrection is the final proof that He had won the victory over death. It just wasn't possible for death to keep hold of Him. Acts 2:24 says - *'God raised* (Jesus) *up, having freed him from the agony of death, because it was not possible that he should be held by it.'*

The resurrection also proved that sin had finally been dealt with and forgiveness won for all by Jesus on the Cross. Romans 4:25 says Jesus – *'was delivered up for our trespasses* (sins)*, and was raised for our justification.'* This means you can be justified before God if you accept Jesus as your Lord and Saviour. You can receive total forgiveness and come into God's presence.

The resurrection means that it is possible, even in this life, to start to live in the victory that Jesus won. Romans 6:4 says – *'just as Christ was raised from the dead through the glory of the Father, so we also might walk in newness of life.'*

Ephesians 2:6 says something amazing. It says that God - *'raised us up with him, and made us to sit with him in the heavenly places in Christ Jesus.'* When you become born-again, that is you accept Jesus as your Lord and Saviour, you are actually spiritually raised with Jesus in heaven. This isn't easy to understand, but it is so wonderful!

When Jesus eventually went back to heaven, He sent His Holy Spirit to live in everyone who is born-again. The amazing truth is that the power that raised Jesus from the dead can live in you. Romans 8:11 says – *'If the Spirit of him who raised up Jesus from the dead dwells in you, he who raised up Christ Jesus from the dead will also give life to your mortal bodies through his Spirit who dwells in you.'* Yes, that power can live in you. It isn't a physical power, but a spiritual one which can work in you and through you in every area and aspect of your life. Ephesians 1:19-20 calls it – *'the exceeding greatness of his power toward us who believe, according to that working of the strength of his might which he worked in Christ, when he raised him from the dead, and made him to sit at his right hand in the heavenly places.'*

When He came back to life Jesus's body had been transformed into a new resurrection body and in 1 Corinthians 15:20 the Bible says that the same will happen to every born-again Christian's body one day - *'Christ has been raised from the dead. He became the first fruits of those who are asleep.'* In other words, what happened to Jesus can happen to you.

The resurrection confirms everything which Jesus won on the Cross. It validates it. Without it there would be no Christianity. It is essential to believe in the resurrection to be born-again and have eternal life with God. God won so much for you through Jesus's death and resurrection, but its blessings and power will only start to operate in your life when you are born-again.

Happy Easter!

'Happy' hardly seems an adequate word to describe such a wonderful, powerful day. So when someone says "Happy Easter" to you, remember just exactly why it is so happy – Jesus, the Son of God rose from the grave and made it possible for you to live with Him in joy and peace forevermore!

The Bible Account

In part 4, I have again combined all the details of Jesus's resurrection into one narrative so you can read the full account in one place.

Part 4

Full Bible Account

The Resurrection

The Full Bible Account of Jesus's Resurrection and Appearances

Matthew 28:1-18
Mark 16:1-18
Luke 24:1-50
John 20:1-31, 21:1-25
Acts 1:2-8
1 Corinthians 15:5-7

Full Bible Account – The Resurrection

Introduction

At the Jews' insistence, the Romans have crucified Jesus, and his body has been laid in a tomb with a huge stone rolled across the entrance to seal it.

The Stone is Rolled Away
Matthew 28:2-4

Behold, there was a great earthquake, for an angel of the Lord descended from the sky, and came and rolled away the stone from the door of the tomb and sat on it. His appearance was like lightning and his clothing white as snow. The Roman guards were so afraid of him that they shook and fell to the ground like dead men.

The Women Arrive at the Tomb
Matthew 28:1,5-8; Mark 16:1-8; Luke 24:1-8; John 20:1-2

Now when the Sabbath was past, on the first day of the week, Mary Magdalene went early to the tomb while it was still dark, and saw the stone had been taken away from the entrance. So she ran and found Simon Peter and John, the disciple whom Jesus loved, and said to them, "They have taken away the Lord out of the tomb, and we don't know where they have laid him!"

At early dawn, Mary the mother of James, Salome, Joanna and other women came to the tomb bringing the spices which they had prepared, that they might come and anoint Jesus. They were saying among themselves, "Who will roll away the stone from the door of the tomb for us?" for it was very big. Looking up, they saw that the stone was already rolled away from the tomb.

They went into the tomb, and didn't find the Lord Jesus' body. While they were greatly perplexed about this, two men stood by them in dazzling clothing. One was a young man sitting on the right side, dressed in a white robe. The women were amazed. Terrified, they bowed their faces down to the earth. The angel said to the women, "Don't be afraid or amazed, for I know that you seek Jesus, the Nazarene, who has been crucified. Why do you seek the living among the dead? He is not here, for he has risen, just like he said. Come, see the place where the Lord was lying. Remember what he told you when he was still in Galilee, saying that the Son of Man must be delivered up into the hands of sinful men, and be crucified, and the third day rise again?" They remembered his words. "Go quickly and tell his disciples and Peter, 'He has risen from the dead, and behold, he goes before you into Galilee; there you will see him, as he said to you.' Behold, I have told you."

They went out, and fled quickly from the tomb, trembling with fear as well as great joy and astonishment. They said nothing to anyone; for they were afraid.

Peter and John Go to the Tomb
Luke 24:12; John 20:3-10

When Mary Magdalene had told Peter and John about the empty tomb, they got up, went out and ran together to the tomb. John outran Peter, and came to the tomb first. Stooping and looking in, he saw the strips of linen cloths lying by themselves, but he didn't enter in.

Then Simon Peter came, following him, and entered into the tomb. He saw the linen cloths lying there, and the cloth that had been on his head, not lying with the linen cloths, but rolled up in a place by itself. So John, who came first to the tomb, also entered in and he saw and believed. As yet they didn't know the Scripture, that Jesus must rise from the dead. So the two disciples went away again to their own homes, wondering what had happened.

Jesus Meets with Mary
Mark 16:9-11; John 20:11-18

Mary Magdalene was standing outside the tomb weeping. As she wept, she stooped and looked into the tomb, and she saw two angels in white sitting, one at the head and one at the feet, where the body of Jesus had lain. They told her, "Woman, why are you weeping?" She said to them, "Because they have taken away my Lord, and I don't know where they have laid him." When she had said this, she turned around and saw Jesus standing there, but she didn't know that it was him. Thus he appeared first to Mary Magdalene, from whom he had cast out seven demons.

Jesus said to her, "Woman, why are you weeping? Who are you looking for?" She, supposing him to be the gardener, said to him, "Sir, if you have carried him away, tell me where you have laid him, and I will take him away." Jesus said to her, "Mary." She turned and said to him, "Rabboni!" which is to say, "Teacher!" Jesus said to her, "Don't hold me, for I haven't yet ascended to my Father; but go to my brothers, and tell them, 'I am ascending to my Father and your Father, to my God and your God.'"

Mary Magdalene went to the disciples and found them mourning and weeping. She told them that she had seen the Lord, and that he had said these things to her. When they heard her say that he was alive, and had been seen by her, they didn't believe it.

Jesus Meets the Women
Matthew 28:8-10; Mark 16:9-11; Luke 24:9-11

As the other women, returning from the tomb, went to tell his disciples, Jesus met them, saying, "Rejoice!" They came and took hold of his feet, and worshipped him. Then Jesus said to them, "Don't be afraid. Go tell my brothers that they should go into Galilee, and there they will see me."

They ran to bring his disciples word and told all these things to the eleven, and to all the rest. Now along with Mary Magdalene, there were Salome, Joanna, and Mary the mother of James and other women who told these things to the apostles. These words seemed to them to be nonsense, and they didn't believe them.

The Chief Priests Bribe the Soldiers
Matthew 28:11-15

Now while the women were going to the disciples, some of the guards came into the city and told the chief priests all the things that had happened. When the chief priests were assembled with the elders, and had taken counsel, they gave a large amount of silver to the soldiers, saying, "Say that his disciples came by night, and stole him away while you slept. If this comes to the governor's ears, we will persuade him and make you free of worry." So the soldiers took the money and did as they were told. This saying was spread abroad among the Jews, and continues until today.

Jesus Appears on the Road to Emmaus
Mark 16:12-13; Luke 24:13-35

After these things Jesus was revealed in another form to two of his followers. They were going that very day on their way into the country to a village named Emmaus, which was sixty stadia from Jerusalem. They talked with each other about all of these things which had happened.

Full Bible Account – The Resurrection

As they walked and talked and questioned together, Jesus himself came near, and walked with them. But their eyes were kept from recognising him. He said to them, "What are you talking about as you walk, and are sad?" One of them, named Cleopas, answered him, "Are you the only stranger in Jerusalem who doesn't know the things which have happened there in these days?" He said to them, "What things?" They said to him, "The things concerning Jesus, the Nazarene, who was a prophet mighty in deed and word before God and all the people; and how the chief priests and our rulers delivered him up to be condemned to death, and crucified him. But we were hoping that it was he who would redeem Israel. Yes, and besides all this, it is now the third day since these things happened. Also, certain women of our company amazed us. Having arrived early at the tomb, and not finding his body, they came and told us that they had also seen a vision of angels, who said that he was alive. Some of us went to the tomb, and found it just like the women had said, but they didn't see him."

He said to them, "Foolish men, and slow of heart to believe in all that the prophets have spoken! Didn't the Christ have to suffer these things and to enter into his glory?" Beginning from Moses and from all the prophets, he explained to them in all the Scriptures the things concerning himself.

They came near to the village where they were going, and he acted like he would go further. They urged him, saying, "Stay with us, for it is almost evening and the day is almost over." He went in to stay with them.

When he had sat down at the table with them, he took the bread and gave thanks. Breaking it, he gave it to them. Their eyes were opened and they recognised him and he vanished out of their sight. They said to one another, "Weren't our hearts burning within us, while he spoke to us along the way, and while he opened the Scriptures to us?"

They rose up that very hour and returned to Jerusalem and found the eleven gathered together and others with them, and told them, "The Lord is risen indeed, and has appeared to Simon!" They related the things that happened along the way, and how he was recognised by them in the breaking of the bread. But the disciples didn't believe them, either.

Jesus Appears to Ten Disciples
Mark 16:14; Luke 24:36-48; John 20:19-23

In the evening on that day, the first day of the week, ten of the eleven disciples were assembled and the doors were locked for fear of the Jews. As they talked, Jesus himself stood among them in the middle, revealing himself to them as they sat at the table. He said to them, "Peace be to you." But they were terrified and filled with fear, and supposed that they had seen a spirit.

He rebuked them for their unbelief and hardness of heart, because they didn't believe those who had seen him after he had risen. He said to them, "Why are you troubled? Why do doubts arise in your hearts?" When he had said this, he showed them his hands and his side and said, "See my hands and my feet, that it is truly me. Touch me and see, for a spirit doesn't have flesh and bones, as you see that I have."

While they still didn't believe for joy, and wondered, he said to them, "Do you have anything here to eat?" They gave him a piece of a broiled fish and some honeycomb. He took them, and ate in front of them. He said to them, "This is what I told you while I was still with you, that all things which are written in the law of Moses, the prophets and the psalms concerning me, must be fulfilled."

Then he opened their minds, that they might understand the Scriptures. He said to them, "Thus it is written, and thus it was necessary for the Christ to suffer and to rise from the dead the third day, and that repentance and remission of sins should be preached in his name to all the nations, beginning at Jerusalem. You are witnesses of these things."

The disciples therefore were glad when they saw the Lord. Jesus therefore said to them again, "Peace be to you. As the Father has sent me, even so I send you." When he had said this, he breathed on them, and said to them, "Receive the Holy Spirit! If you forgive anyone's sins, they have been forgiven them. If you retain anyone's sins, they have been retained."

Thomas Doubts
John 20:24-25

But Thomas, called Didymus, one of the twelve, wasn't with them when Jesus came. The other disciples therefore said to him, "We have seen the Lord!" But he said to them, "Unless I see in his hands the print of the nails, and put my hand into his side, I will not believe."

Jesus Appears to All Eleven Disciples
John 20:26-29

After eight days again his disciples were inside, and Thomas was with them. Jesus came, the doors being locked, and stood in the middle, and said, "Peace be to you."

Then he said to Thomas, "Reach here your finger, and see my hands. Reach here your hand, and put it into my side. Don't be unbelieving, but believing." Thomas answered him, "My Lord and my God!" Jesus said to him, "Because you have seen me, you have believed. Blessed are those who have not seen, and have believed."

Jesus Appears to Over 500 Followers
1 Corinthians 15:5-7

After Jesus had appeared to Peter and the other disciples, he appeared to over five hundred brothers at once, most of whom remain until now, but some have also fallen asleep. Then he appeared to James.

Full Bible Account – The Resurrection

Jesus Appears to Seven Disciples
Matthew 28:16; Luke 49:50; John 21:1-14

After these things, the eleven disciples went into Galilee. Jesus led them out as far as Bethany. He revealed himself again to the disciples at the sea of Tiberias.

It was this way. Simon Peter, Thomas called Didymus, Nathanael of Cana in Galilee, the sons of Zebedee and two others of his disciples were together. Simon Peter said to them, "I'm going fishing." They told him, "We are also coming with you." They immediately went out, and entered into the boat. That night, they caught nothing.

But when day had already come, Jesus stood on the beach, yet the disciples didn't know that it was him. Jesus therefore said to them, "Children, have you anything to eat?" They answered him, "No." He said to them, "Cast the net on the right side of the boat and you will find some." So they cast it and now they weren't able to draw it in for the multitude of fish. John said to Peter, "It's the Lord!"

When Simon Peter heard that it was the Lord, he wrapped his coat around him (for he was naked), and threw himself into the sea. But the other disciples came in the little boat (for they were not far from the land, but about two hundred cubits away), dragging the net full of fish. When they got out on the land, they saw a fire of coals there and fish laid on it, and bread. Jesus said to them, "Bring some of the fish which you have just caught." Simon Peter went up, and drew the net to land full of great fish, one hundred and fifty-three; and even though there were so many, the net wasn't torn. Jesus said to them, "Come and eat breakfast." None of the disciples dared inquire of him, "Who are you?" knowing that it was the Lord. Then Jesus came and took the bread, gave it to them, and the fish likewise. This is now the third time that Jesus was revealed to his disciples, after he had risen from the dead.

Jesus Reinstates Peter
John 21:15-19

When they had eaten their breakfast, Jesus said to Simon Peter, "Simon, son of Jonah, do you love me more than these?" He said to him, "Yes, Lord; you know that I love you." He said to him, "Feed my lambs." He said to him again a second time, "Simon, son of Jonah, do you love me?" He said to him, "Yes, Lord; you know that I love you." He said to him, "Tend my sheep." He said to him the third time, "Simon, son of Jonah, do you love me?" Peter was grieved because he asked him the third time, "Do you love me?" He said to him, "Lord, you know everything. You know that I love you." Jesus said to him, "Feed my sheep. Most certainly I tell you, when you were young, you dressed yourself, and walked where you wanted to. But when you are old, you will stretch out your hands, and another will dress you, and carry you where you don't want to go." Now he said this, signifying by what kind of death Peter would glorify God. Then he said to him, "Follow me."

Peter Asks About John
John 21:20-23

Then Peter, turning around, saw John following. This was the disciple whom Jesus loved, the one who had also leaned on Jesus' breast at the supper and asked, "Lord, who is going to betray You?" Peter seeing him, said to Jesus, "Lord, what about this man?" Jesus said to him, "If I desire that he stay until I come, what is that to you? You follow me."

This saying therefore went out among the

brothers that this disciple wouldn't die. Yet Jesus didn't say to him that he wouldn't die, but, "If I desire that he stay until I come, what is that to you?"

Jesus Does Many Signs
John 20:30-31,21:24-25; Acts 1:3

After he had suffered Jesus proved himself alive to his disciples many times, appearing to them over a period of forty days, and speaking about God's Kingdom. He did many other signs and things in the presence of his disciples which are not written in this book; which if they would all be written, I suppose that even the world itself wouldn't have room for the books that would be written. But these are written, that you may believe that Jesus is the Christ, the Son of God, and that believing you may have life in his name. The disciple, John, testifies about these things, and wrote these things. We know that his witness is true.

Jesus Commissions His Disciples
Matthew 28:16-18; Mark 16:15-18; Luke 24:49; Acts 1:2,4-8

The eleven disciples went to the mountain where Jesus had sent them and Jesus came to them. When they saw him, they bowed down to him. Being assembled together with them, through the Holy Spirit he commanded the apostles whom he had chosen, "Don't depart from Jerusalem, but wait for the promise of the Father, which you heard from me. For John indeed baptized in water, but you will be baptized in the Holy Spirit not many days from now."

They asked him, "Lord, are you now restoring the kingdom to Israel?" He said to them, "It isn't for you to know times or seasons which the Father has set within his own authority. Behold, I send out the promise of my Father on you. But wait in the city of Jerusalem until you are clothed with power from on high. You will receive power when the Holy Spirit has come upon you."

And he spoke to them, saying, "All authority has been given to me in heaven and on earth. Go into all the world, and preach the Good News to the whole creation. He who believes and is baptized will be saved; but he who disbelieves will be condemned. These signs will accompany those who believe: in my name they will cast out demons; they will speak with new languages; they will take up serpents; and if they drink any deadly thing, it will in no way hurt them; they will lay hands on the sick, and they will recover. You will be witnesses to me in Jerusalem, in all Judea and Samaria, and to the uttermost parts of the earth."

Part 5

Understanding Christianity Booklet

Why Jesus Went Back to Heaven

When Jesus went back to heaven, it marked the end of His life and work on earth.

Jesus on Earth

He had been born as a baby in a humble situation. His mother was a virgin called Mary and this meant He was fully human, but He was conceived miraculously by God and this meant that He was fully God too. He wasn't half human and half God, but fully both.

When He grew up, He fulfilled all the Old Testament prophecies which had been spoken about the Messiah hundreds of years before. He healed the sick and the disabled, He brought people back to life, He delivered people, He brought them into spiritual freedom, and He taught them about the Kingdom of God, what it is like and how to become part of it.

He was put to death on a Cross. As He died, He took all the weight and shame of sin on Himself – all that everyone has done, is doing, or ever will do wrong. He suffered God's anger and all the punishment people deserve Himself, so that they wouldn't have to suffer it. He also took all the sickness and poverty of this world on Himself and won the victory over it all. He did it for everyone – He did it for you.

On the third day after His death, He came back to life and spent more time with His followers, helping them to understand all that had happened and explaining to them how they should spread His wonderful news to the rest of the world.

The Ascension

After a while, Jesus returned to His Father God in heaven, demonstrating that He had completed everything that God had sent Him to do on earth. He returned to the glory He had left behind when He was born as a humble baby on earth. This is called the Ascension.

And in heaven God restored His glory to Him and sat Him at His right hand, the place of honour. God confirmed that His name was the Name above every name - higher, more important, significant and powerful than any other. Philippians 2:9-10 says – *'Therefore God also highly exalted him, and gave to him the name which is above every name; that at the name of Jesus every knee should bow, of those in heaven, those on earth, and those under the earth.'*

Glory

There is a description of Jesus in glory in heaven in Revelation 1:12-16. It is part of a vision which God gave to John, one of Jesus's close followers – *'I saw seven golden lamp stands. And among the lamp stands was one like a son of man, clothed with a robe reaching down to his feet, and with a golden sash around his chest. His head and his hair were white as white wool, like snow. His eyes were like a flame of fire. His feet were like burnished brass, as if it had been refined in a furnace. His voice was like the voice of many waters. He had seven stars in his right hand. Out of his mouth proceeded a sharp two-edged sword. His face was like the sun shining at its brightest.'* We don't know if this is an accurate description or if it is a way of trying to express what can't be expressed. But it speaks of glory unimaginable.

What a Contrast!

It is amazing to compare the glory of Jesus in heaven with the humility of a little baby born in a place where animals ate, and brought up in a humble family in an insignificant town. It shows how immeasurable God's love for people is, that Jesus was willing to leave all that glory behind to live humbly on earth. Philippians 2:5-8 says – *'Have this in your mind, which was also in Christ Jesus, who, existing in the form of God, didn't consider equality with God a thing to be grasped, but emptied himself, taking the form of a servant, being made in the likeness of men. And being found in human form, he humbled himself, becoming obedient to death, yes, the death of the cross.'*

This is true sacrificial love and it was all for you. It was for everyone, but also for each individual person – Jesus made that sacrifice because He loves you so much. He'd have done it for you if you were the only person on earth.

To Start His Work as High Priest

In the Old Testament, long before Jesus was born, God had set up a system where the people could only approach God through a priest and the High Priest would approach God on their behalf. He was a person chosen by God and set apart for this work.

But through His death, Jesus opened the way for everyone to be able to approach God personally and directly. The place where God's presence dwelt in the Jewish temple was called the Holy of Holies. It was separated from the rest of the temple by a very tall curtain. Only the High Priest was allowed to go into the Holy of Holies and only once a year.

When Jesus died the curtain was miraculously ripped from top to bottom, showing dramatically that anyone and everyone could now approach God directly – they no longer needed to go through a priest. A one-on-one relationship with God was now available to everyone who would believe. You can go straight into God's presence because Jesus has opened up the way.

Jesus became the eternal one-and-only High Priest and He had to return to heaven so He could begin this new work. Hebrews 4:14 says – *'Having then a great high priest, who has passed through the heavens, Jesus, the Son of God.'* Jesus is not a High Priest in that you have to go to Him and tell Him what you want to say to God and He then talks to God for you. No – He has opened up the way for you personally to go directly to God as well as to Himself.

As High Priest, Jesus is interceding for you. Romans 8:34 says – *'It is Christ who died, yes rather, who was raised from the dead, who is at the right hand of God, who also makes intercession for us.'* This doesn't mean He is pleading with God to be merciful to you. God has already shown you complete mercy through Jesus dying in your place. And He's not trying to persuade God that you deserve blessing - no-one does deserve it and no-one could ever earn it - it's impossible. But Jesus's presence before God in heaven, with the wounds of His torture and death on His body, stands as a continual proclamation of all He has won for you through the Cross, including your total forgiveness.

To Prepare a Place for You

Jesus said in John 14:2 that when He was back in heaven He would prepare a place for believers to live in after their death - *'In my Father's house are many homes. If it weren't so, I would have told you. I am going to prepare a place for you.'*

When you accept Jesus as your Lord and Saviour you become born-again. This means that when you die on earth, you will then live forever in heaven in joy and peace with God. And Jesus is getting your home ready for you.

The Bible says that born-again Christians will share in Jesus's glory. Romans 8:17 says — *'if indeed we suffer with him, that we may also be glorified with him.'* If you believe that Jesus is

Lord and that He died for you and personally accept that He suffered the guilt, shame and punishment in your place, then glory will be yours! So this home isn't going to be just something functional that will do. Jesus is the ultimate architect, builder and interior designer! You're going to love your home in a way you can't even imagine now. It's going to be perfect – just right for you!

So Believers Can Be in Heaven Too

Ephesians 2:6-7 says that God - *'raised us up with him, and made us to sit with him in the heavenly places in Christ Jesus.'* Notice the verb 'made' is past tense. In some amazing way that can't really be explained, the spirits of born-again believers are already in heaven with Jesus!

So the Holy Spirit Could Come

Jesus also explained to His followers that He had to return to heaven so that His Holy Spirit could be sent to all believers. John 16:7 says – *'Nevertheless I tell you the truth: It is to your advantage that I go away, for if I don't go away, the Counsellor* (Holy Spirit) *won't come to you. But if I go, I will send him to you.'*

When Jesus was here on earth he could only be in one place at a time because He was limited physically as a human being. But once He had returned to heaven, His Spirit could be released and live in everyone who is born-again at the same time. His Spirit is a person just as He is, and is called 'He' not 'It'.

Christians call His Spirit the Holy Spirit or the Holy Ghost, but He isn't a ghost as we think of that term - He is the very nature and presence of Jesus. So when Jesus went back to heaven, He wasn't abandoning His followers – He'd promised that He would never leave them. But He would be with them in a different way. Through His Holy Spirit He would live in each one of them personally and individually forever.

Jesus told His followers to wait for the Holy Spirit to give them power before they started spreading the news of Jesus to others. He said in Acts 1:4-5 – *'Don't depart from Jerusalem, but wait for the promise of the Father, which you heard from me ... you will be baptized in the Holy Spirit not many days from now.'* And in Acts 1:8 He said – *'you will receive power when the Holy Spirit has come upon you. You will be witnesses to me in Jerusalem, in all Judea and Samaria, and to the uttermost parts of the earth.'*

And this is what happened following His ascension. One day, while His followers were all together, Acts 2:2-4 says – *'Suddenly there came from the sky a sound like the rushing of a mighty wind, and it filled all the house where they were sitting. Tongues like fire appeared and were distributed to them, and one sat on each of them. They were all filled with the Holy Spirit, and began to speak with other languages, as the Spirit gave them the ability to speak.'* Jesus's followers now had spiritual power to spread the news of Jesus to others, rather than having to do it in their own strength.

The Holy Spirit comes to live in everyone when they're born-again. But God wants you to experience the full potential of the power of the Holy Spirit to help you live your life. There won't be flames of fire on your head and probably not a rushing wind, but if you ask Him, God will release the power in His Holy Spirit in you. Wow!

To Show How He Would Return

Jesus's close followers were there when Jesus went back to heaven. They saw it happen with their own eyes. Acts 1:9 says – *'as they were looking, he was taken up, and a cloud received him out of their sight.'* It goes on to say in Acts 1:10-11 – *'While they were looking steadfastly into the sky as he went, behold, two men stood by them in white clothing, who also said, "You men of Galilee, why do you stand looking into the sky? This Jesus, who was received up from you into the sky will come back in the same way as you saw him going into the sky.'* The ascension demonstrated the way Jesus will return one day when He will come, not as a humble baby, but coming down from heaven in all His glory to finally set up His Kingdom on earth.

Good News!

The whole of Jesus's life, teaching, miracles, death, resurrection and ascension is called the gospel which means good news. What wonderful good news it is that Jesus returned to heaven, not leaving His followers lost and abandoned, but releasing His presence, power and understanding to them and in them through His Holy Spirit. And it's all available to you too right now because He is in heaven – good news indeed!

The Bible Account

Part 6 is the last of these full Biblical accounts, describing exactly what happened at Jesus' ascension.

Part 6

Full Bible Account

The Ascension

Mark 16:19-20
Luke 24:51-53
Acts 1:9-11

Full Bible Account – The Ascension

So then the Lord, after he had spoken to them, lifted up his hands, and blessed them. While he blessed them, as they were looking, he withdrew from them, and was taken up, and a cloud received him out of their sight. He was received up into heaven, and sat down at the right hand of God.

While they were looking steadfastly into the sky as he went, behold, two men stood by them in white clothing, who said, "You men of Galilee, why do you stand looking into the sky? This Jesus, who was received up from you into the sky will come back in the same way as you saw him going into the sky."

They worshipped Jesus, and returned to Jerusalem with great joy, and were continually in the temple, praising and blessing God. Amen.

Part 7

How to be Born-Again

When you acknowledge that Jesus is God and decide that you want to follow Him you are making Him your Lord. If you've never accepted Jesus as your Lord and Saviour then make today the day you do. God loves you totally and unconditionally, but it's only as you're born-again that He becomes your Father and you are able to experience that wonderful love relationship with Him.

Romans 10:9 says - *'if you will confess with your mouth that Jesus is Lord, and believe in your heart that God raised him from the dead, you will be saved.'* Tell God you are sorry for the wrong things you do, say and think. Believe that Jesus is Lord, that He died for you and that He is now alive. Accept Him as your Lord and Saviour. Say it with your voice and believe it in your heart.

If you've done that sincerely, you are now born-again. Jesus has come to live in you and your spirit has been made brand new - believe it and thank Him. Everything you've ever done wrong or ever will do wrong is forgiven, and you will be with God for eternity.

As a child of God you have lots of brothers and sisters – a whole new family. And you have the Bible, God's Word to you, which will help you understand and experience more of His love.

It was All for You

Everything Jesus won through the Cross and His resurrection and His ascension is for you. Whatever your life has been like or is like, Jesus died for you and rose from the dead for you, and went back to heaven for you. Accept Him and start to see things change for the better as you set out on your new exciting life with Jesus, knowing that God loves you so much that He sent His Son to die in your place so that you could live forever with Him. Yes, the Cross is for you, the resurrection is for you and the ascension is for you – isn't that wonderful!

For God so loved the world,
that he gave his one and only Son,
that whoever believes in him
should not perish,
but have eternal life.
(John 3:16)

Jesus said
'I came that they may have life,
and may have it abundantly.'
(John 10:10)

If you will confess with your mouth
that Jesus is Lord,
and believe in your heart
that God raised him from the dead,
you will be saved.
(Romans 10:9)

All my booklets are on my website.
You can read them online
or download and print them out
completely free of charge.
There is no limit to the number of copies you may
print for your own use or to give away.

www.understandingchristianity.co.uk

Titles include –

Be Transformed
God Loves You
God's Not Angry With You
Spirit, Soul and Body
The Cross Changed Everything
Who is the Holy Spirit?
What about Suffering?
God Wants You To Be Well
I Can Today Because of Jesus
Free Indeed!
Forgiveness
From Darkness Into Light
It's All About Grace

I am adding new booklets regularly.

Katherine Hilditch

Printed in Great Britain
by Amazon.co.uk, Ltd.,
Marston Gate.